Candidates
Of
Bewitchment

Dr. D. K. Olukoya

Candidates of Bewitcment

© *FEB.* 2012 - CANDIDATES OF BEWITCHMENT
DR. D. K. OLUKOYA

ISBN: 978-978-920-006-1

THE BATTLE CRY CHRISTIAN MINISTRIES
322, Herbert Macaulay Way, Sabo, Yaba,
P. O. Box 12272,
Ikeja, Lagos.
Website: www.battlecryng.com
Email: sales@battlecryng.com
Phone: 08033044239 - 018044415

I salute my wonderful wife, Pastor Shade, for her invaluable support in the ministry.

I appreciate her unquantifiable support in the book ministry as the cover designer, art editor and art adviser

All rights reserved. Reproduction in whole or part without written permission is prohibited.

All scripture is from the King James Version.

Cover illustrated by: Sister Shade Olukoya

CONTENTS

CHAPTERS		PAGES
1	CANDIDATES OF BEWITCHMENT	5
2	HIGHER FOOLS	18
3	LIBERTY WITHOUT FREEDOM	38

Chapter 1
Candidates of Bewitcment

Candidate of bewitchment

This book contains God's urgent message for you. The fact that He has preserved your life up till this time means that He has a purpose for it.

Act 8:9-13.

But there was a certain man, called Simon, which beforetime in the same city used sorcery, and bewitched the people of Samaria, giving out that himself was some great one: To whom they all gave heed, from the least to the greatest, saying, This man is the great power of God. And to him they had regard, because that of long time he had bewitched them with sorceries. But when they believed Philip preaching the things concerning the kingdom of God, and the name of Jesus Christ, they were baptized, both men and women. Then Simon himself believed also: and when he was baptized ,he continued with Philip, and wondered, beholding the miracles and signs which were done.

Later, the secret of Simon was revealed and it was known that he was a sorcerer.

A GLOBAL PROBLEM

Many people and many nations are being bewitched. The Lord has a controversy with many people because they are not walking the way He wants them to walk. Many people go to churches to get themselves entertained instead of getting their spirit man changed. Many are working below God's standard. Such people must do something before God turns away from them because bewitchment is a terrible thing and it has assumed an epidemic proportion.

Many people now are behaving just like the Samaritans in the Scriptures above. The people of Samaria were under so much suffering but they never realised it. They were under blindness and satanic elusion but they did not know. They praised the very man who was destroying them. They did not really know who Simon was. He was sapping them dry but they believed he was delivering them.

It is the same thing with a lot of people. They do not know whom they are dealing with and what such people do at night. They are just being sapped dry. Simon was destroying them properly and thoroughly but satan made sure they were blind to it.

This is not a time to be spiritually blind, so you better pray off the blindness now. The people of Samaria ignorantly hailed their enemy. They called their friends, enemies and called their enemies friends. This is what we call bewitchment.

SPIRITUAL MANIPULATION

A lot of people invest their money where they are not

supposed to and they have been losing. Some put their legs where they should not put them and are licking their wounds now. In Samaria, destruction had already settled over them, sadness was everywhere in the city; unclean spirits had already possessed so many people. Nevertheless, they went about normally. They dressed in three - piece suits and went about like respected men and women although they were bewitched.

Successful businessmen and politicians of Samaria were all blinded by the devil. There were sicknesses in the land, but it never bothered them. There were unclean spirits everywhere, almost in every home, yet they felt strangely normal. They thought Simon was the answer to their problems whereas he was the problem. Slowly and ironically, they were dying and praising the man who was sinking their boat.

What was happening in Samaria? Bewitchment. They were bewitched, but however, all of a sudden, the Holy Spirit located Simon and declared him a satanic agent. We have a lot of people going about looking normal and respectable, but inside, they are bewitched.

WHAT DOES IT MEAN TO BE BEWITCHED?
It means to be spiritually influenced by the power of witchcraft. It is casting a spell on people. You find a lot of people burying live cows and some eating raw

animals to bewitch others and they succeed in caging so many people. That is the bewitching power of the devil. It is when a person has been captured like this that he cannot move ahead again. Although he is making motions, he is not making any progress.

Examine your life to see the dark areas of your heart that the light of God has not touched. A lot of negative things are manifesting in the dark regions of people's lives. Except they allow these dark regions to be reached by the fire of the Holy Ghost, they would continue to be bewitched. They urgently need to work on these areas of their lives that are still bewitched.

Perhaps, you have been allowing sin to bewitch you and God has been warning you, talking to you, and even making some trouble to come your way so that you can sit up, yet you hold on to the sin. A prophet of God is telling you that sin is a viper and that it will certainly kill, but something makes you to continue in that sin and to remove your eyes from the effect of the bewitchment. All the "I don't know what made me to do it," is the work of bewitchment.

Bewitchment paints sin in attractive colours and makes it respectable. Things like pride, drunkenness, indiscipline, rebellion, lying, dishonesty, homosexuality, gossiping, promiscuity, laziness, drug addiction, belonging to one cult or the other, adultery, prostitution, all are evidence of bewitchment.

WHO IS A BEWITCHED PERSON?

1. A bewitched person is a person who stubbornly clings to sin, in spite of warnings.

2. A young man of 17yrs was brought to us for prayer. When he removed his clothes, there were sores all over his body, including his reproductive organ. But in spite of all the sores, he still continued in his immorality. That was bewitchment.

3. He is a person who has been blinded by the devil and cannot even see that the devil has been defeated.

4. He is one who has been kept away from using his or her divine weapons. Galatians 3:1 says: "O foolish Galatians, who hath bewitched you, that ye should not obey the truth, before whose eyes Jesus Christ hath been evidently set forth, crucified among you?"

   These Galatians were going to church but were Bewitched all the same.

5. He is a person operating under the destructive effect of sin.

6. He is a person suffering from mind confusion. If you notice that your mind is always confused, you cannot put things together or when you do and it gets to the edge of success, something goes wrong, know that there is bewitchment in place.

7. He is a person who exhibits stubborn disobedience to God's command.

8. He is a person who makes unexplainable mistakes. Such a person cannot explain why he does certain things, and cannot justify his actions. When a professor begins to make the kind of mistakes that someone who is uneducated should not make, you know that he is bewitched.

9. He is a person operating under different powers that are beyond his control.

10. He is a person who does not know what happens to his or her money. He or she just knows that the money comes in but does not know what is happening to it. It is bewitchment.

Candidate of bewitchment

Sometime ago, a millionaire, who had lost everything he had in a mysterious way, came for prayers. The Holy Spirit revealed that it was his daughter that destroyed his money. So, I asked him to bring her. He brought her and she confessed that she used witchcraft means to lock up his money. And that one of her aunties was her accomplice. The man had money but did not know what happened to it - Bewitchment.

11. He is somebody who has completely lost the joy of the Christian life, that is, the joy of salvation.

12. He is somebody who is struggling against a force he cannot understand and cannot master. A lot of people struggle with what they do not understand, It is bewitchment. Just like the people of Samaria who went deeper and deeper into what was destroying them.

THE GOOD NEWS

The good news is that Jesus came and was manifested in the flesh. The Creator was made a creature. It was a fantastic process of humility. Jesus who was clothed in glory now wore rags of the flesh. He, whose glory filled the heavens and the earth, was now carried into a cot in a manger because He wanted to deliver us from bewitchment.

He, the God of circumcision, was circumcised. The one, who owns the earth and the fullness thereof, got to a level where He said, "I am hungry, I am thirsty." The God of life was put to death. The One that said, "I and the Father are one," now cried, "My God, my God, why hast thou forsaken me?" In His lifetime, He had no where to lay His head.when he died, no place could contain his body.

The King of kings was punished, a crown of thorns was placed on His head. His holy ears listened to the blasphemies of men; His face was spat upon, His back was beaten, His hands of power that came on the sick and the sick recovered were nailed to the cross. His soul was forsaken on the cross. Why? So that the whole of the bewitching power of satan, of sin and of the world would be broken, so that the light of God can shine into the darkness of our lives, So that the enemy does not bewitch us anymore. That facility is still open now for those who want to take advantage of it. Nowadays, a lot of people go to the market and never come back. Some go to buy refrigerators and end up inside the refrigerators. A lot of terrible things are happening in the world today but God has better things for us. If we will put away our sins, come to repentance, humble ourselves so that God can speak peace into every situation of our lives, our lives would be changed for the better.

You have an opportunity to receive the touch of God in a mighty way and for all the bewitchment of the past years in your life to completely disappear so that you can start a new life. If only you can seize this wonderful opportunity.

SIN

Sin says: "I don't care about what God is saying, I don't care about God's commandments. I prefer to please myself than to please Him. I am going to be the Lord of myself." it is not moved by the blessings and gifts of God. It makes one to treat the Almighty God with contempt. The music of sinners is: "I don't care what God requires, I must have my own way. I refuse to submit to the authority of God. I don't care what God Almighty has threatened to do. I am not afraid. His eyes may be upon me but I am not going to be restrained, I don't care what He wants and what He hates. I shall please myself." That is the music of sinners. But God is asking for repentance today. Where there is no Holy Spirit, there is failure. Do not allow your life to remain the same after reading this book.

> *2 Chronicles 7:14 says:*
> *"If my people, which are called by my name, shall humble themselves, and pray, and seek my face, and turn from their wicked ways; then will I hear from heaven, and will forgive their sin, and will heal their land."*

You must turn away from any evil pattern that you have been following. If you have not made peace with God, you must do so now and repent completely. If there are 50 leakages in a ship and you block 49, the one left can still sink the ship. So your repentance must be total. God does not want you to be serious today and unserious tomorrow. He does not want you to go back to your vomit. This is the message He has for you as you move on in life.

A lot of people are under the power of bewitchment. They are being controlled by the powers they do not understand and they cannot see the spiritual powers controlling their environments. Many do not recognise that the fellow they are sitting with in the office may be calling on another thing to undo or subdue them. It is bewitchment. At this juncture, I want you to make this declaration out loud with holy anger: "Bewitchment must die, in the name of Jesus."

Christian life is not for entertainment. It is for you to possess your possession. Therefore, I encourage you to give your life to Christ if you have not done so, because you cannot defeat bewitchment except by the power in the blood of Jesus.

HOW TO GIVE YOUR LIFE TO CHRIST AND BECOME A CHILD OF GOD

1. **Admit that you are a sinner:** "For all have sinned and come short of the glory of God" (Romans 3: 24).

2. **Repent:** "Repent ye therefore and be converted that your sins may be blotted out" (Acts. 3: 19).

3. **Confess:** "If we confess our sins, He is faithful and just to forgive us our sins, and to cleanse us from all unrighteousness" (1 John 1: 9).

4. **Forsake:** "Let the wicked forsake his way, and return unto the Lord, and He will have mercy upon him" (Isaiah 55: 7).

5. **Believe:** "For God so loved the world, that he gave his only begotten son, that whosoever believeth in him should not perish, but have everlasting life. " (John 3: 16).

PRAYER POINTS

1. I dismantle every satanic agenda programmed against me this week, in the name of Jesus.

2. **Point your fingers to the heavens and say this:** I speak unto the sun, the moon, and the stars to favour me this week, in the name of Jesus.

3. **Point to the earth and say this:** Anything programmed against my life in the earth, I dismantle you by fire, in the name of Jesus.

4. Every evil kingdom reigning against my life, I overthrow you, in the name of Jesus.

5. Every plan of the enemy for my life this week, I dismantle you, in the name of Jesus.

6. I raise the whirlwind of the Lord, to pursue every stubborn pursuer, in Jesus' name.

7. I raise the thunder of the Lord to pursue every stubborn pursuer, in Jesus' name.

8. Lord, advertise your power in my life, in the name of Jesus.

9. This week, you must co-operate with my destiny, in the name of Jesus.

10. Let the programme of my life be enforced upon the enemy, in the name of Jesus.

11. Bewitchment must die, in the name of Jesus.
    Isaiah 40:31 says:

Candidate of bewitchment

Chapter 2
Higher
FOOL

Isaiah 40:31 says: *"They that wait upon the Lord shall renew their strength. They shall mount up with wings like the eagle. They shall run and not be weary. They shall walk and not faint"*

There is power to build up and there is power to pull down. But the best power is the power from on high, which will make you to mount up like the eagle. That is the kind of power that we should ask for. There are some Christians whose names have been taken to the dark places by the evil ones and they succeeded. But some other names were taken there and the satanic agents said, "Sorry, we cannot touch these ones. It is impossible."

There are fools and there are fools. When you say that somebody is a fool, perhaps you mean that he is silly and does not think very well or that he has a poor sense of judgment. The question is: who is the best person to describe a fool? If a fellow human being calls you a fool, you may have nothing to worry about, but if God calls you a fool, you must be really foolish.

WHO ARE FOOLS?

This is the first thing we are going to look at before we see who the higher fools are.

> *Psalm 107:17 says:*
> *"Fools because of their transgression and because of their iniquities are afflicted. Their soul abhoreth all manner of meat: and they draw near unto the gates of death."*

Here, fools are people who are being afflicted because of their transgression and they do not know that it is because of their transgression. They are unable to locate the fact that their problem started as a result of the sins in their lives.

The Bible says that they are foolish because they refuse to know that the reason why they are going through what they are going through is their transgression. Having failed to repent of their transgression, trouble started.

> *Proverb 1:7 says:*
> *"The fear of the Lord is the beginning of knowledge: but fools despise wisdom and instruction."*

This means that the beginning of knowledge is not 'A' for Apple, 'B' for Ball and 'C' for Carrot, but the fear of the Lord. The Scripture goes ahead to say: "But fools despise wisdom and instructions." When somebody who knows more than you is talking, who has passed through experiences and has the Spirit of God in him, you will be a fool not to listen to him.

Proverb 1:22 says:
"How long ye simple ones, will ye love simplicity? And the scorners delight in their scorning and fools hate knowledge?"

Here, fools are described as those who despise knowledge and correction, they are those who hate knowledge and follow their own opinions.

People all over the world, no matter where they come from, have the choice of three authorities to operate under.

1. **Personal opinion:** The first authority is your own opinion. If you begin to say things like, "Well, it's my own opinion, it is my own opinion," and you believe that your own opinion is right while other people's opinions are wrong and that your own opinion about Christianity is the only correct one, then perhaps, you will be the only one to go to heaven and you will be very lonely there.

You may say, "Preacher, what if what you are saying here is wrong too?" If it is wrong, it then means that Jesus is not the King of kings and the Lord of lords after all, because the word of God is straightforward. Everything having to do with the salvation of man is

Candidate of bewitchment

well spelt out. The Bible makes itself plain and clear. It says, "He that committeth sin is of the devil." It does not put any middle class. It does not say, "Those who commit little or minor sins." Pastor, apostle, evangelist or whatever you call yourself, once you commit sin, you are of the devil. Committing sin means that you are taking sides with the enemy of God.

When Jesus came, He was not ready to listen to people's opinions. He was not ready to listen to the truth of others, because He is the truth. You may also say, "What if you are wrong too?" Well, I still prefer my lifestyle to a lifestyle outside Christ. Someone may say, "Well, I don't know whether Jesus is the King of kings and the Lord of lords. I don't know whether there is hell or there is heaven." Well, I don't lose anything because I know that heaven and hell exist and that Jesus is the Kings of kings and the Lord of lords. Those who fail to believe this will lose because when they die they will discover that the same Jesus that they have rejected is the King of kings.

Sometime ago, two groups of people argued whether God exists or not. The first group said that He existed, while the second group said that He did not. The group that said that God did not exist asked questions like: "If actually God exists, why does He permit motor accidents? Why does He permit people to die anyhow, and children to die in hospitals, and all kinds of evil things happen? There is definitely no God." The second group who said that God existed would say, "Well, the things that we find in the world make it unreasonable to say or believe that God does not exist. It appears there is one intelligent brain behind all these things, and that intelligent brain is what people call God."

These two groups argued for a week and many Christians backslid during the debate. On the last day, their professor, a white man, who was to conclude the debate came and made the following statement: "It is more logical to believe that God exists because if you say that He does no exist, and you die and discover that He exists, He will deal with you." That closed the debate. So, some people are labouring under their own opinions, and that is one authority.

2. **Other people's opinion:** Another authority is other people's opinion, which may be right or wrong. These are the things that control our lives. You may say, "No" but this is true. If everybody were blind and could not see, many of us would change our dressing. Some people who paint parts of their body like masquerades and do all kinds of things will stop when they discover that nobody admires them. They will not even bother to wear bathroom slippers to work. So, people also labour under other people's opinion.

3. **God's opinion:** The highest opinion is that of the Almighty God and His Book. The devil has no opinion. He has a mission and his mission is to destroy.

> *Proverb 12:15 says*
> *"The way of a fool is right in his own eyes: but he that hearkeneth unto counsel is wise."*

It means that a fool is a person who is always right in his own eyes, and immediately you begin to correct him, you hurt him, you hurt his feelings.

> *Proverb 28:26 says: "He that trusteth in his own heart is a fool: but whoso walketh wisely, he shall be delivered."*

So, one whose ways are right in his own heart, is a fool according to God. For example, the Bible's order of marriage is just twofold. It says, "Wives, be subject to your husbands, and husbands, love your wives." If people will just obey these two instructions, there will be no problem. "Wife be subject to your husband" means that if as a wife you are stating your opinion and your husband opens his mouth and says, "Shut up," you should respect him and keep quiet.

If you are not ready to do that, you should not have got married, you need not have dropped your father's name to pick up another man's own. If people will obey this, many homes will remain standing. If you say, "Well, I studied Biology in the University," So what? Do you marry Biology? Your insistence that "I must talk, I am educated, I have my own opinions," would only break the home into pieces. Most of the people asking you to talk and return fire for fire will later be laughing at you and saying, "He has thrown her out."

A fool is always right in his own heart. Drop your opinion and follow what God is saying. When there is no subjection, love does not follow. It is just like Christ and His church. If you refuse to subject yourself to the leadership of Christ, there will be problem for you.

> *Proverb 14:9 says:*
> *"Fools make a mock at sin: but among the righteous, there is favour."*

THE FOLLY

It means that fools take sin lightly and forget the words of the Bible. If the Son of God, the 'water of life' could suffer so much for Him to say, "I thirst, give me water," and instead of being given water, He was given vinegar, And He cried out in pain and God watched it happen, then woe unto that preacher or that Christian who would take sin lightly. This is why God is withdrawing His children from the dead churches. He shed His blood for them and will not allow them to perish in those dead places. His blood cannot go in vain; His children must be set free.

> *Proverb 16:5 says:*
> *"A fool despiseth his father's instruction: but he that regardeth reproof is prudent."*

Children who despise their father's instructions are fools.
The Bible says that their days will not be long.

THE CURSE

I know a man who is a lawyer and his father too was a lawyer. He was very rude to his father. He thought he was a good match for his father because they were both in the same profession. One day, the father said to him, "What you are doing to me, your children will do to you in future." The man replied, "That is rubbish, shut up." The man later died. And After the death, the young man started having problems.

When he wanted to marry, he was manipulated into marrying the highest witch in the city. Right from the first night after the wedding, when both of them slept on the bed, the bed was turning around in circles and continued so until daybreak. He used to urinate once or twice at night, but with the circling around of the bed he began to bed wet. When they woke up, his wife would say to him, "Useless man, I did not know that you are like this. After messing up now, you will put on your suit and go to argue in the court. One day, I will go to the court and tell them that you bed-wet."

With this kind of manipulation, the wife became the husband and the man became the wife because he was afraid that they would find out that he was bedwetting. One day, he went to court to defend someone. It was as if the judge woke up on the wrong side and everything he said was termed rubbish. After sometime, everything went wrong in the court and he was ordered to be kicked out. And right from there, things ceased to work well for him.

LEARNED FOOLS

One day, he met a preacher who said to him, "God said, you have offended somebody and you need to make a restitution." He said, "The only person I know I quarrelled with was my father." The preacher asked after the father and he told him that he had died. The preacher told him how serious the matter was and the man then begged God to forgive him. He went straight to the grave of his father and wept and wept for almost six hours asking for forgiveness. God saw him and said, "Ok, I forgive you." But somebody does not have to pass through all that. Although he was a lawyer, learned men as they are called, as far as the Bible is concerned, he was a fool.

Knowledge is different from wisdom. Education is different from wisdom. The fact that you attended school and passed your examinations does not mean that you are wise. The Bible calls such people fools.

> ***Proverb 20:3 says:"It is an honour for a man to cease from strife: but every fool will be meddling."***

It says that they will be meddling, they will be fighting until people would say, "Are those two people not Christians and we see them carrying the Bible." The Bible calls them fools. The Bible says, "Be quick to hear, but be slow to speak." Most times, when you keep your mouth shut, people will not know that you are a fool, but it is when you start talking that they will know. You will expose yourself.

Sometime ago, two sisters were fighting and people ran to the mission house to call the pastor. The pastor came on his bicycle and said, "It is okay." One of them said to the pastor, "Oga, this is not church. This is a personal thing. I cannot, because I am born again, become a tablemat. So, Mr. Pastor, when I come to church, you can talk. This place is our house." And she continued fighting. She is a fool, according to the Bible.

> *"A brutish man knoweth not; neither doth a fool understand this."* **Psalm 92: 6**

THE HOUR OF DELIVERANCE

It is my earnest prayer that any fool reading this message will receive deliverance, in Jesus' name. And all those whose eyes have been blinded to the truth of God's word shall be set free, in Jesus' name.

> *Proverbs 18:6-7*
> *"A fool's lips enter into contention, and his mouth calleth for strokes. A fool's mouth is his destruction and his lips are the snare of his soul."*

All wrong users of the mouth are fools, according to the foregoing. proverbs 26:11:

> *"As a dog returneth to his vomit, so a fool returneth to his folly."*

All backsliders who have refused to slide back to Jesus are fools.

The next class of fools is in the book of Ecclesiastes 7, which says,

> *"Be not hasty in the spirit to be angry: for anger resteth in the bosom of fools."*
> Ecclesiastes 7: 9

Angry people are regarded as fools by God. If you still get angry, then you are a student in the school of foolishness, and you must depart quickly from that school.

HIGHER FOOLS

Psalm 14 :1 says
"The fool has said in his heart, there is no God. They are corrupt, they have done abominable works, there is none that doeth good."

The Bible says that the fool says in his heart, and not that he speaks it out. He does not talk, he is just thinking it and yet the Bible says that he is a fool. If the Bible could call somebody who is thinking that there is no God a fool, how about the one who is saying it? That one must be a higher fool.

We have a lot of people today who keep saying that there is no God. It is not their fault. If they were to be alive before the gospel came into this land, they would understand better. Before the gospel came to this land nobody wore good clothes and came out. If one did, witches would eat him up the next day. Only a few people who were strong could do that.

THE DARKNESS

If you have not read about the darkness that prevailed in Africa before the gospel came, please, do so. Demons were walking in the streets in the daytime. They were not hiding in the night. In some places in this country, witches were flying in the afternoon. But now, they dare not try it. A small child of God can now point his little finger and command fire to come down. It was not so before, because in those days many people did not know that there was fire anywhere.

> *LUKE 24:25 says*
> *"O fools and slow of heart to believe all that the prophets have spoken: ought not Christ to have suffered these things and to enter into his glory?"*

At a stage, Jesus described His own disciples as fools because of their sluggishness in understanding spiritual things.

> *LUKE 12:16-21 says:*
> *"And he spake a parable unto them saying, The ground of a certain rich man brought forth plentifully: And he thought within himself, saying, What shall I do, because I have no room where to bestow my fruits? And he said, This will I do, I will pull down my barns and build greater; and there will I bestow all my fruits and my goods. And I will say to my soul, Soul, thou hast much goods laid up for many years; take thine ease, eat, drink and be merry.*

> *But God said unto him, Thou fool, this night, thy soul shall be required of thee: then whose shall those things be, which thou hast provided? So is he that layeth treasure up for himself, and is not rich toward God."*

These are the highest fools. The Bible also says, in *Deuteronomy 32::29:*

> *"O that they were wise, that they understood this, that they would consider their latter end"*

This is saying that when a man is wise, he would not be thinking of the immediate profit. So, everyone who lives and dies without making adequate preparation about where he or she is going is a fool.

When last did you think about heaven? Where are the rich men of yesterday? Where are the popular ones? Have you not forgotten them. In a few years to come, the children that will be born will not know some names that are popular now, unless they read about them. Sooner or later, many people who have been doing great things will become "Ex this and Ex that." You have to plan to heaven.

TRUE RICHES

You have to be rich towards God. A lot of people are busy doing only what is convenient for them. Don't do what is just convenient for you. If the service is not convenient for you, you do not come. It is better not to have been born than to have been born and you fail to make eternity, or you are unprepared for death.

Birth is your opportunity, it is your beginning from where there is no returning. Once you have been born, you cannot say, "Mummy, I don't like the world. Oh, let me go back into your womb." No, it is impossible. Death, too, is a commitment from which there is no escape. At birth, we all commence the journey from this world to the next. You cannot turn back from the journey. Only the body is the creature of this earth. It is therefore utter foolishness for any man to presume that he can find his way to God on his deathbed. God gives no such guarantee to anybody.

GOD'S RULES

Sometime ago, in England, I was made the head of a Bible study group in a particular hall. We held our Bible study on Tuesdays. The first day I taught, I found that many people felt uncomfortable. The next time I was to talk, immediately I entered the study room, I found that somebody had ironed some clothes there. We did not know that the sister we were to hold the Bible study in her room was getting ready to go for a party with an unbeliever. She was just waiting for us to complete the Bible study.

I started to talk by saying, "Well, God will meet you the way death meets you and there is no guarantee that in the next five minutes, you will still be here. Those who still patch their Christianity, who are not yet ready to stand out, are planning for destruction because when Jesus was around, He was very rigid.

So, in case you are looking for somebody who will bend the rules, not the Lord Jesus Christ. Jesus Christ kept saying woe to the enemies of the gospel. He called the Scribes and the Pharisees the sons of those who killed the prophets. But He spoke good words unto those who loved Him. As we closed the Bible study, the sister said, "Daniel, wait, I want to talk with you. What you said today is just what I needed to shake me out of my slumber. But, you see, I am a young girl, you are old. How do I enjoy myself. You can afford not to go to disco but me, a young girl, how will I get on."

SUDDEN DEATH

Then I opened to Psalm 119: 9 which states how the young should live their lives. I made her to understand that what she called enjoyment was not enjoyment but destruction coated with sugar. When you finish eating the sugar, the bitterness would enter into your mouth. A lot of people are like that and we call them chameleon Christians. It is very risky not to be sure of heaven because an unexpected accident can suddenly throw someone into hell or heaven to spend eternity there.

One man of God used to say, "Sudden death, sudden glory." That was because he was ready for death. Someone who is not ready cannot say that. If you are not rich towards God, you cannot say that. Nobody is born into the way of Christianity. The fact that you were born into a Christian home does not automatically make you a Christian. Christianity has to be understood. It is a way. The Bible says, "Seek and you shall find." You have to find the way and move therein. If you neglect this opportunity that God presents to you is as if you are rejecting his grace.

If you persist in unbelief, and refuse to respond to God's call, it is spiritual suicide. One of the most worrying verses in the Bible, which many people wish that it were be removed. 1 peter 4:17-18 which says

> *"For the hour is come that judgment must begin at the house of God: and if it first begin at us, what shall the end be of them that obey not the gospel of God? And if the righteous scarcely be saved, where shall the ungodly and sinner appear."*

Consider the fact that the righteous shall scarcely be saved. Think about it. Ask questions like, "What am I doing here? Where am I going? When I die, what will happen?" If you have never thought about these, then you need serious prayers.

THE GLUE

When you are tied to the world, it will glue you. When the trumpet sounds, it will glue you down. The church is in the world, but the world should not enter into the church. This deceptive world we are living in will sink one day and those who are not ready to separate from it, shall sink with it. Many Christians are too worldly-minded to be heavenly wound. The world is constantly seeking to defile the child of God and if you allow it, it will have its way.

Today, I want you to think about it very well. There is a small part of electricity network called a fuse. The current passes through it. When God looks at you and sees that the fuse in your life has blown, no matter how powerful your environment may be and fire is coming out, it won't enter you. Some people have inferior fuses and cannot carry any power. Such people should really cry unto the Lord.

One of the greatest tragedies of Christianity is the rearrangement of priorities. Many Christians are very active when they are praying against their enemies whereas the Bible says, "Seek you first the kingdom and all other things shall be added." It means that those things will be pursuing you and not you pursuing them.

PRAYER POINTS

1. Lord, lay your hand upon my life and make my life a miracle, in the name of Jesus.

2. Lord, give me the power to mount up with wings like the eagles, in the name of Jesus.

3. I refuse to become the serpent's meat, in Jesus' name.

4. Lord, anywhere my name is called for evil, let fire and thunder fall there, in the name of Jesus.

5. I command the Red Sea to swallow all my Pharaohs, in the name of Jesus.

Chapter 3
Liberty Without Freedom

In John 11, we see one of the most interesting stories in the Bible. The friend of Jesus had been sick. and They called him but He did not show up until four days after the man had died.

John 11: 38 -44 saya:

"Jesus therefore again groaning in himself cometh to the grave. It was a cave, and a stone lay upon it. Jesus said, Take ye away the stone. Martha, the sister of him that was dead saith unto him, Lord, by this time he stinketh: for he hath been dead four days. Jesus saith unto her, Said I not unto thee, that, if thou wouldest believe, thou shouldest see the glory of God? Then they took away the stone from the place where the dead was laid. And Jesus lifted up his eyes, and said, Father, I thank thee that thou hast heard me. And I knew that thou hearest me always: but because of the people which stand by I said it, that they may believe that thou hast sent me. And when he thus had spoken, he cried with a loud voice, Lazarus, come forth. And he that was dead came forth, bound hand and foot with grave clothes and his face was bound about

*with a napkin. Jesus saith unto them,
Loose him, and let him go."*

LOOSE HIM

Lazarus was raised from the dead by the power of God. Likewise all that believe in Christ have been given a new life. They have been lifted out of the graveyard of sin and sorrow. Jesus said, "Loose him and let him go." It means that he could not go unless they loosed him. Although Lazarus was raised from dead, he was still bound. He experienced liberty but not freedom. Captivity was over but he was still bound. The grip of death upon his life had been broken but he was still bound. It is a double tragedy that many believers are still walking around with grave clothes on.

There are children of God who speak in tongues but are still bound. They have their grave clothes on like Lazarus. Jesus has set them free but they are still in their grave clothes. This is the sad condition of many people today. A lot of Christians are still bound by their past failures, past sins, guilt and materialism.

Many believers are bound by traditions, that is why you see Christians going for chieftancy titles and they allow evil people access to their heads which are the symbols of their destiny.

Many believers are still bound by bad habits. Lazarus was alive but constrained; he could see, but through a veil; he could hear but not clearly. Why? He was still in grave clothes. So, perhaps you have been born again for years and you still cannot see, it means that something is blinding your spiritual eyes. You have to pray for the grave clothes to be pulled off. Remember when Saul preached in a particular place and the people fought and argued that he was speaking lies, he said, "I have one last thing to tell you before I leave.

Remember that what is happening to you is what was written by the prophets that behold, you wander and you perish, for it is written I will send my words unto them, but hearing they will hear but they will not understand, they will behold but cannot see. Their heart is already hardened so that my hands cannot deliver them, so that they can perish." With that Paul concluded the sermon.

If you have read through the whole of the Bible and decided to continue to be evil, a popular passage in the book of Revelation says, "Continue," and if you want to continue to do good, it says, "You may continue. But behold, I come quickly and my reward is with me, and my reward can be bad or good, to give to every man according to the works of his hands."

EVIDENCE OF GRAVE CLOTHES

Many people go to churches where they do not understand the language which their leaders speak. After the meetings, they come out, bring out their cigarettes and begin to smoke. As far they are concerned, they are serving the Lord. That is bondage. Also, sex outside marriage is evidence that a person is bound in grave clothes. A believer who is working with a fake certificate is bound in grave clothes. Obtaining sick leave papers when you are not sick is an indication that you are in grave clothes. Sleeping and pretending to be praying is a sign of being in grave clothes.

If you are the worst of human beings when you are angry, you are in grave clothes. Masturbation, chronic impatience, and constant fear are evidence that there are grave clothes on. That is why Jesus said, "Loose him and let him go." The Lord said the same thing to Pharaoh. Unforgiving spirit, sexual sins and failure to break all connections with the devil are evidence of grave clothes.

You claim to be born again but still keep complimentary cards of your former boy friends, it means that the grave clothes are still on. If not, why are you keeping them? Failure to confess every sin, envy, backbiting, and not yielding every area of your life to God are evidence of grave clothes.

If God is your lover and you believe the Bible, which says that your Maker is your husband, you will not be in a hurry to get out from His presence. So, rushing out of the service without sharing the grace is an evidence of grave clothes. Not having on the whole armour of God means there are grave clothes on.

THE CARNAL NATURE

The truth is that the percentage of those who are ready for the rapture is very small. Many people who saw visions of the rapture but did not go up discovered that it was as a result of grave clothes on them. Grave clothes can be in the form of hair and other body attachments.

A certain man was in a very big trouble. He was sacked from five jobs. When he could not feed his family again, his wife ran away, leaving him with three daughters. To worsen his sorrow, his first daughter became pregnant while in form three. When he tried to beat her, she said, "Daddy, all the time I did not ask you for bus fare to school. Where do you think the money I was spending came from?" The man was very sad, so he cried unto the Lord in prayers.

He really cried to God and you know God never ignores the cry from the heart. The Lord Jesus appeared to him while he was praying. The man was very happy. He wanted the Lord Jesus to sympathise with him. For God to promote him and give him deliverance from all his troubles. He wanted comfort, fairness and divine justice. But to his amazement, the Lord pointed at him and said, "Your problem is rooted in you and not in the enemy."

The Lord told him that such was the hardest part of his Christian life. "You have not even agreed that you are your own problem. You are only deceiving yourself by blaming the devil. I am the Almighty. I am not struggling with the devil. I desire that your flesh must submit to me. I want to dethrone you from the centre of your life and be your Lord, but you have not allowed me to do so.

You must contend with this power of your flesh, which is hindering my work and preventing me from doing what I want to do in your life," the Lord said. The man was surprised but for the first time he got the blunt truth, which they say, is sometimes very bitter. You see, the devil is not really the issue as much as the power of the flesh. It is the flesh that is hanging grave clothes onto the bodies of many people.

> *Galatians 5:17 says:*
> *"For the flesh lust against the spirit, and the spirit against the flesh and these are contrary the one to the other, so that ye cannot do the things that ye would."*

The flesh is fighting against the spirit and the spirit is fighting against the flesh. Two of them are contrary so that you cannot do the things you are supposed to do. Here lies the secret of victory against any form of satanic attack. Here lies the victory for you to make heaven without anybody pulling you down. If a dry fast is declared for seven days in the church, what do you think will happen? Some people will protest loudly. Some would say, "Do you not know that we would go to work?" Some would say, "They want to kill people in this place." Others would say, "I have been telling you about that church. You see, now they want seven days dry fast." That is the power of the flesh. They forget that there is something called the bread of heaven. Once you eat that one, you lose the desire to eat the one that is here on earth.

THE FLESH

If for example you go on three days dry fast, you will find out that by the third day even if someone is abusing you, you will not able to talk too much. The secret of that is that Mr. Flesh has been weakened. That is the value of fasting. It does not change God, it is you that has to change, because the flesh lusts against the spirit and the spirit too lusts against the flesh. The two of them are always fighting. When you begin to starve one, say the flesh, your spirit man now becomes stronger. That is the value of fasting. You can pray with more concentration, with more fire, and then you get result.

God has issued a death sentence on Mr. Flesh: "Dust thou art and unto the dust thou shall return." It is the spirit man inside you that will return to God. The flesh knows that it is not going to depart from the dust and it wants to pull you along if you allow it.

THE DOOR

The devil comes in when we open the door to him through our uncrucified flesh. So our toughest battle is not with the devil, it is with the flesh. The devil is continually looking for open doors through which he can enter to attack us.

John 14:30:
"Hereafter I will not talk much with you for the prince of this world cometh, and hath nothing in me."

There was no place in the flesh of Jesus that the devil could have access to. Jesus was dead to Himself. He was dead to His own desires and His own agenda.

The power of darkness operate the most powerful scanning machines. As you are now, they can see you clearly in and out. They know whether any part of them is in you. They know how strong you are; they know those who are spiritual and those who are not. They know those who pray in the morning before going out, they know those who do not pray. They know those who do their quiet time and those who do not. They know those who are merely warming the benches in the church, who are not really serious with the Lord.

THE LURE OF COMPROMISE

They know those who are in the church to look for good, obedient, submissive wives, and they know those who are looking for very brilliant and rich husbands. They can detect the smallest compromise. They know the cleverly concealed sin. They know the evil habits you are covering. That is why the day of judgment would be very interesting. There are many things we do not know now, but on that day, everything will be made manifest.

Jesus made one statement: "That which was done under the bed shall be proclaimed on housetops." The person will be shouting it; he will have a megaphone and will be shouting it and everybody will know what he has covered. Those things inside your heart which the gentle voice of the Holy Spirit is saying, "Son this is not good, daughter this is bad," and you ignore His voice, those are the grave clothes. With them you have liberty but not freedom.

How can a believer go and buy clothes on credit. If she puts on the clothes she will not pass the front of the shop of the person who sold it to her for fear of the person saying, "You see the clothe that woman is wearing, she has not paid for it." It is the grave clothes. Why don't you wash the ones you have, keep them clean and wear them?

THE UNCRUCIFIED FLESH

The devil defeats Christians who celebrate an uncrucified flesh. The devil defeats Christians who leave the doors of their lives open to him. He is looking for houses to dwell in. He is looking for landing spaces and any area of a person's life can be his landing space if you submit to him.

Mr. Flesh can completely paralyse the destiny of somebody if he submits any part of his life to him. If you submit your hair, he will grab it. If you submit your head, he will grab it if you submit your thought, he will grab it, if you submit your marriage, he will grab it. If you submit your sex life, he will grab it, if you submit even ordinary fingernail, he will grab it. There are some people now who have stopped cutting their fingernails and they are as long as those of the vultures and they paint them.

Some people buy and put on extra nails and paint them with mermaid colours. Then they start writing to us that they need deliverance from spirit husbands. May be you did not know, just like physical men find some women very attractive, there are spirits that find some women very attractive. Those are the spirits who go about at night violating women and sexually harassing them. We should not make their job easy. Immediately you are dressing to make their job easy they will visit you.

The church is a house of God, a holy place, not a place you come wearing transparent dresses; or you are a man, you open your shirt and show the chain you put on for all to see. If you come before God you should submit and humble yourself.

SATANIC LIPS

If you submit your lips to the enemy he will grab it. The number of men of God who hear from God clearly is reducing because of polluted ears. If you submit your ears to the enemy, he will grab them. If you submit your mouth to the enemy, he will grab it. If you submit your job to him he will grab it. If your kind of job requires that you tell lies every time, you better look for another job before you end up in hell fire. Pray to God to provide you another job where you will not be telling lies. If you submit your eyes to the enemy, he will use it. If you give him your ambition, he will use it. If you give him your certificate, he will use it. If you give him your voice, he will use it. Most of those singing worldly songs that would send people to hell fire were trained by the church, but they are now used by the devil.

Galatians 5:24 says:
"And they that are Christ's have crucified the flesh with the affection and lusts."

So, if you find that the enemy is strengthening himself against you, the area to check is your flesh. The thief in you must die. The hypocrisy in you must die, and the iniquity in you must die, so that the Spirit of God can use your life as He wants.

THE CRUCIFIXION

They that belong to Christ must crucify the flesh with its affection and lust. That is, if you do not belong to Christ, you can live your life the way you want. But at the end of the day, you will arrive at the gate of life and the gate-keeper will say, "We don't have your name here. You are our enemy. Get out, you worker of iniquity." You may say, "Well, I will be doing it little by little." The danger with little by little is that you do not know the day the Lord will say, "Son, it is enough. Come home." What we are saying is that Mr. death does not give an advance notice.

Somebody brought money to Peter and said, "Take this money, and give me this gift so that whoever I pray for will receive the Holy Spirit and will be speaking in tongues." Peter looked at him and said, "Your money perish with you." That is, there was nothing in Peter that would respond to that sensation and temptation for money.

Peter allowed God to crucify that area in his life. But this is the area where the flesh is on the throne in many lives. The Bible says that we came to the world with nothing and that we will go away with nothing. You came to the world fasting and you will go back with an empty stomach. Why should you glue yourself to this sinking world, because you do not want to crucify the flesh.

CARNAL ENERGY

The flesh is anything that is not energised by the Holy Spirit and is always fighting you. You want to read your Bible, it says, "sleep." You want to pray and that would be when somebody will annoy you and you spend two hours fighting. You want to pray and it is that time they bring a vampire movie and you begin to watch. Many Christians engage in activities not ordained by the Holy Spirit. To get rid of our grave clothes, the bottom-line is that God should rule our flesh. Do not deceive yourself. Do not think that the flesh will improve, it cannot improve. It is rotten to the core.

Many of the problems we have as individuals are caused by Mr. Flesh. For example, inability to take the right decisions, plain disobedience to God, looseness with the opposite sex, emotional problems, bad thinking, boiling anger, etc. we must take responsibilities for our own lives. When you say, "Mr. Flesh, die," heavens will rejoice, and they will come to your aid. If you have not pointed your finger to yourself and say: "It is you that annoyed me. You made me to say this, you made me to say that," you are not serious yet. But the day you point the accusing finger to yourself, heaven will rejoice and will come to your aid.

THE LORD

Our most difficult problem is facing ourselves. In 1979, one brother prayed and said that one sister was his wife. The pastor invited him and the sister and said to the sister: "This brother has prayed and he says you are his God's chosen wife." The lady looked at the pastor and looked at the brother from head to toe and said, "Sorry, pastor, this one that is sitting down beside you cannot carry my load." The pastor said, "Which load are you carrying that he cannot help you to offload." She said, "Pastor, that is my decision. That is what I want to do and that is it." Up to this moment that sister is still looking for somebody to help her carry that load.

> *Philippians 3:3 says:*
> *"For we are the circumcision, which worship God in the spirit, and rejoice in Christ Jesus, and have no confidence in the flesh."*

There should be no confidence in the flesh, for the flesh is dangerous and has no mercy. The flesh is harder to deal with than the devil.

You cannot bind your own flesh. So it is the harder problem, which it needs to be crucified. Self-centredness, lack of discipline, boasting and stubbornness are nothing more than the flesh refusing to submit to the Holy Spirit. Many churchgoers are very stubborn. A stubborn person will say, "I will do it in my own way." But the Bible says, "Woe unto those that are at ease in Zion." It also says, "If you walk with footmen and you are weary, what will you do when you are asked to walk with the horsemen?"

NO CONFIDENCE

It is the foot men that are around now but eventually they will go and the horse riders will come in, and things will get worse because that is what the Bible says. Evil men shall wax stronger and stronger and peace will disappear, unless we welcome the Prince of peace and the Lord of lords.

Everyday, we come across people who are trying to train Mr. Flesh more and more. They want to train Mr. Flesh not to overeat. They want to train their minds to think right but they cannot train the flesh, because the Bible says, "Those that are after the flesh do mind the things of the flesh, they that are after the spirit do mind the things of the spirit." The flesh cannot please God. It cannot because it is in enmity with God. It is in contention with the Spirit of God and cannot fight the spiritual battle which we do everyday.

HOW DO WE OVERCOME THE FLESH?

1. **Leave no place for the flesh. Romans 13:14 says:**
"But put ye on the Lord Jesus Christ, and make not provision for the flesh, to fulfil the lust thereof."

Do not make provision for the flesh. When you plan to buy extra clothes that you do not need, when you plan to buy extra food you will not eat, when you plan to watch a video film that you know will bring lust into your life, when you are meditating on what to say to hurt another person, then you are making provision for the flesh.

Make life hard for the flesh. When next it says, "Do not greet so and so," go and buy a gift, look for the person, greet the person and give him the gift. When you do that, you are killing Mr. Flesh. You are not giving it provision to operate. When you, a single girl follows a man you do not know to somewhere; when you, a woman asks for a ride from an unknown man, you are making provision to cause trouble for yourself.

You know that you used to be a palm wine drinker. Now you are born again, do not accompany anybody to the place again so that the smell will not enter into your spirit. If you go there it means you are making provision to commit sin again.

> *That is what Romans 13:14 says.*
> *But put ye on the lord Jesus Christ, and make not provision for the fresh, to fulfil the lists there of*

2. **Bring the flesh under subjection.** We are to make the flesh a slave to God.

    I Corinthians 9:27 says:
    "But I keep under my body, and bring it into subjection: lest that by any means, when I have preached to others, I myself should be a castaway."

The Bible says that no man can serve two masters. You cannot walk down two roads at the same time. You cannot walk in the way of holiness and in the way of sin.

You have to put the flesh under subjection. What does it mean to bring it under subjection? To ignore its advice and suggestions, tell it all the time that you are the Chairman, so it has to take your own instructions. When it says, "Go and do this," you disobey and do the opposite. When it says, "Can't you notice that when this one is passing she does not greet anybody, so any time she is coming just turn your face away," you should now do the opposite. You greet the person very well.

3. **Put off the old man and put on the new man.**
   Philippians 4:22 says:
   "That ye put off concerning the former conversation, the old man, which is corrupt according to the deceitful lusts."

Put off the coat of the old man and put on that of the new man. You cannot put on two coats at the same time. So, the old man must go and the new man must come in. If your Christianity has not got to the level where somebody says, "Ah, he has changed," you are still a joker.

4. **Deny the flesh.** Jesus said, if any person would come after Him, let him deny himself and take his cross and follow Him.

Matthew 16:14 says:
"If any man or woman will be my disciple let him first deny himself and then follow me."

This means that you have to put Mr. Flesh on the shelf, put it aside. Put your pride aside. If Mr. Flesh says, "They have insulted you, charge at them," you should say, "No, I will not. I have been nailed to the cross."

5. **Mortify your members.**
Colossians 3:1-5 says:
"If ye then be risen with Christ, seek those things which are above, where Christ, sitteth on the right hand of God. Set your affection on things above not on things on the earth. For ye are dead, and your life is hid with Christ in God. When Christ who is our life, shall appear, then shall ye also appear with him in glory. Mortify therefore your members, which are upon the earth; fornication, uncleanness, inordinate affection, evil concupiscence, and covetousness, which is idolatry."

Candidate of bewitchment

If you do not mortify the members of your flesh you are an idol worshipper. You have to focus on what God has already done for us on the cross.

6. **Regard the flesh as crucified and remind it everyday that it is already dead.**
   Galatians 5:24 says:
   "And they that are Christ's have crucified the flesh with the affections and lusts. If we live in the spirit, let us also walk in the spirit."

Paul said, "I am crucified with Christ nevertheless I live but I live now the life of Jesus, Son of God who died for me." The old Paul had been dead many years, the new Paul was walking along the street then. It was the old Paul that a serpent could bite and he would die but the crucified one could not die like that.

7. **The people the devil fears most are those who have crucified the flesh.** He knows he cannot find any entrance in them.

8. **Live an exchanged life.** You should put one life down and take another. According to Galatians 2:20, the new life is to replace the old one. You cannot be doing two things at a time. When you are moving close to the solution and you see your sad condition, you have started making progress. The day a mad

man begins to ask questions like: "Why am I wearing these clothes? What am I doing here? Why are you all starring at me?" The solution to his problem has started. But when he has dirty clothes on and he says, "Give me the iron, I want to iron my clthes," the solution is not in sight yet.

You should now prayer like John Knox. The same God who answered his prayer and made it impossible for demons and the host of hell to paralyse his destiny, is still alive.

PRAYER POINTS
1. Oh God, break me, in the name of Jesus.

2. Oh God, kill the iniquity in my life, in the name of Jesus.

3. Every hindrance to open doors in my life, give way by fire, in the name of Jesus.

4. Spiritual blindness, clear out of my life, in the name of Jesus.

Where others are failing, I shall succeed by fire, in the name of Jesus.

OTHER PUBLICATIONS OF DR. D. K. OLUKOYA

1. 20 Marching Orders To Fulfil Your Destiny
2. 40 Marriages That Must Not Hold
3. 30 Things Anointing Can Do For You
4. 70 Rules of Spiritual Warfare
5. A-Z of Complete Deliverance
6. Be Prepared
7. Bewitchment must die
8. Biblical Principles of Dream Interpretation
9. Born Great, But Tied Down
10. Breaking Bad Habits
11. Breakthrough Prayers For Business Professionals
12. Brokenness
13. Bringing Down The Power of God
14. Can God?
15. Can God Trust You?
16. Command The Morning
17. Consecration Commitment & Loyalty
18. Contending For The Kingdom
19. Connecting to The God of Breakthroughs
20. Criminals In The House Of God
21. Dealing With Hidden Curses
22. Dealing With Local Satanic Technology
23. Dealing With Satanic Exchange
24. Dealing With The Evil Powers Of Your Father's House

25. Dealing With Tropical Demons
26. Dealing With Unprofitable Roots
27. Dealing With Witchcraft Barbers
28. Deliverance By Fire
29. Deliverance From Spirit Husband And Spirit Wife
30. Deliverance From The Limiting Powers
31. Deliverance of The Brain
32. Deliverance Of The Conscience
33. Deliverance Of The Head
34. Deliverance: God's Medicine Bottle
35. Destiny Clinic
36. Destroying Satanic Masks
37. Disgracing Soul Hunters
38. Divine Military Training
39. Divine Yellow Card
40. Dominion Prosperity
41. Drawers Of Power From The Heavenlies
42. Evil Appetite
43. Evil Umbrella
44. Facing Both Ways
45. Failure In The School Of Prayer
46. Fire For Life's Journey
47. For We Wrestle ...
48. Freedom Indeed
49. Holiness Unto The Lord
50. Holy Cry
51. Holy Fever
52. Hour Of Decision

About The Book

Bewitchment has assumed an epidemic proportion now. Unfortunately, a lot of people are ignorant of their true state. They believe that they know what they are doing whereas they have completely lost control of their lives. These individuals hobnob with their own very enemies, and praise those destroying them.

If you are still living below the standard of God for your life, or you are struggling against a force you can neither understand nor master, know that there is bewitchment in place. This book shows you the way of escape.

About The Author

Dr. D. K. Olukoya is the General Overseer of the Mountain of Fire and Miracles Ministries and The Battle Cry Christian Ministries.

The Mountain of Fire and Miracles Ministries' Headquarters is the largest single christian congregation in Africa with attendance of over 120,000 in single meetings.

MFM is a full gospel ministry devoted to the revival of Apostolic signs, Holy Ghost Fireworks, miracles and the unlimited demonstration of the power of God to deliver to the uttermost. Absolute holiness within and without as spiritual insecticide and pre-requisite for heaven is openly taught. MFM is a do-it-yourself Gospel Ministry, where your hands are trained to wage war and your fingers to do battle.

Dr. Olukoya holds a first class honours degree in Micro-biology from the University of Lagos and a PhD in Mulecular Genetics from the University of Reading, United Kingdom. As a researcher, he has over seventy scientific publications to his credit.

Anointed by God, Dr. Olukoya is a prophet, evangelist, teacher and preacher of the Word. His life and that of his wife, Shade and their son, Elijah Toluwani are living proofs that all power belongs to God.

ISBN: 978-978-920-006-1

www.ingramcontent.com/pod-product-compliance
Lightning Source LLC
Chambersburg PA
CBHW060857050426
42453CB00008B/998